A Himalayan Poem

Also by Nishi Chawla

Novels
Twist of Truth
A Human Silicon Chip

Poetry
The Ganga: A River Poem
Confluences I: Indian Women, Indian Goddesses
Confluences II: Indian Men, Indian Gods
Iraq War Memorabilia

Drama
Behind Female Grit and Glory: Three Feminist Plays From South Asia

Non Fiction
Samuel Beckett: Reading The Body in His Writings

A Himalayan Poem

Nishi Chawla

STERLING PAPERBACKS
An imprint of
Sterling Publishers (P) Ltd.
Regd. Office: A1/256 Safdarjung Enclave,
New Delhi-110029. CIN: U22110DL1964PTC211907
Tel: 26387070, 26386209; Fax: 91-11-26383788
E-mail: mail@sterlingpublishers.com
www.sterlingpublishers.com

A Himalayan Poem
Copyright © 2017, Nishi Chawla
ISBN 978 81 207 9470 2

All rights are reserved.
No part of this publication may be reproduced, stored in a retrieval system or transmitted, in any form or by any means, mechanical, photocopying, recording or otherwise, without prior written permission of the original publisher.

Printed in India

Printed and Published by Sterling Publishers Pvt. Ltd.,
Plot No. 13, Ecotech-III, Greater Noida - 201306,
Uttar Pradesh, India

Dedicated to my first grandchild

Aarin

whose name embodies the strength of a mountain.

CONTENTS

Looming	9
Reflecting	25
Snowing	39
Inhabiting	51
Nesting	67
Denuding	81
Meditating	91
Symbolizing	103

ONE

LOOMING

If being tall is being splendid,
You loom large in your largesse.
Rise high and bold. Covered in gleaming
Gold and green, rock brown.

Mighty and majestic, standing tall,
You are the Himalayas! Rock strong,
A blanket of silvered mist covers
Your summits, your rocky life between.

Himavat ruled you, his snow abode where
With his wife, Minavati, he gave birth to
The lovely Ganga, and to the ever nurturing
Parvati. Two daughters, two forms of giving.

Fifteen hundred miles of Devi worship, a vast
Kingdom of mesmerizing meditation, fate deciding
Karma, an experiential reality mixed with Jnana,
Share a portion of the divine, rituals of pure Bhakti.

So Himavat chatted with Parvati, so the hundred
Or more mountains born in sacred shapes, Devi Gita,
All of their peaks crowned, consecrated.
Mount Everest rises, above them, sanctified.

Emerging from their steep inclines, these
Peaks nod, sharply look askance at the haunts
Built by us, poor mortals bent on fissuring,
Mausoleum like, contain the bones.

Touching your northern flanks, the placid
Tibetan plateau breathes free, deep gulps.
To your south lies the regal Gangetic plain,
The soil eroded, then shaped and reshaped.

The Indus and the Ganga shake loose,
Their granular mass, fragments unconsolidated
In their thin, sandy remains. Basins full of
Silted memories. Clayed down, graveled.

Bedrock of chains, meager, mighty,
The Karakorum and the Hindukush nestle
Along your northwest reaches, striated, looming,
Endless signs of caucus lick off the muscles.

Assam lies to your east, its copper skies
Peerless, Bodo land of ground tilts, and
Oceans of green surging, singing, then
Dissolve, its slithering seven sisters.

Spreading southward, a bend in the Indus,
River of my dreams, rippling northerly, attach
Like a heavy western anchor, Nanga Parbat
Dares, climbing its nudeness, freezes.

Will its inner core thaw, will the iced
Ridge rise up like the Mezano wall, curl
Around the valley, drop down Diamir steep,
Leftover for the Gods, Rupal precipice like?

Namcha Barwa is your easternmost side,
Anchor the high ranges in the webbed feet,
Of a bend in the river Tsangpo. The Tibetan
Himalayas soar blue, tipping high.

Then undulate with easy, wave like rhythms,
Dance like the burning thunders of a jealous
God come alive. Tower over the Tsangpo gorge,
Drop, drop down in sheer delight.

Falling down, down, until you shiver
Garnished in multi costumed finery,
Rendered raw, changing with the dark
Rawness of the curious moon.

Between the tall spear piercing the sky
And the sheer drop, down into the river
Rests a vastness. Human imagination floats
In the crevices of myths guarding them.

The Menba and Luoba are ancient folks,
They part from their restless rituals, point
By single point, as the Yarlong Tsangpo
River valley expands, point the music.

Mountain music here rises, from the dark
Eastern depths of the Tsangpo gorge, a dis-
Quieting deep, where time stands still. Only
Its music ensues. Chant like, visceral.

Music that moves, soul captions of
The deepest cavern, it soars and it dips,
Uncanny laughter ensues, though there is
No straight flat line here for miles.

Mount Namche Barwe is where the
Soul explores its own lost music. Beneath
The shadow of that music, sad yet fervent,
It feels too high to touch its own shadow.

If a churning, if a music can be created out
Of a collision, pulsing and surging between
Two tectonic plates, crush and break into
A fifteen hundred mile long mountain arc.

Decline its head, a section of the earth
Becomes estranged; lumbers, lumpishly
Contorted and deformed, as if its throat was
Cold by the lateral compression.

Orogeny is like a dance, the jewel
Of the youngest range. Kindling
New love into triangular stars.
Uplifted, metamorphosed, sedimented.

Rock like, an ocean gathers around it,
Declines its head, Tethys gets buried. Lost
In the soft waters, the volcanoes fringing,
Like antiques that are thrust faulted.

The art of composing a continental thrust,
Middle passages govern, subduct into
An oceanic trench, designed to tighten
Around the body of the mantle, then rise.

The plate pushes under the plateau,
Like a whisper rising to a scream
Like a convergence, a visionary company
A seismic encroachment, to fling.

So you will rise higher, pulse by
Pulse, the angelus of thrusts, heaping,
Growling in geological activity, nor
Barren, neither abated. Move upward.

You have witnessed ice sheets
Compressed with pure rage. There you spread
Along your northern edges, crooked
Neighbor of my dreams, my dread.

An ice stream of glaciers dotted,
Lines that connect, hail and climb
An instant, a network in the Karakoram,
Jagged, outflow of my cold dreams.

Between the Kanchenjunga to the east,
Now and in time to stick; a glacier stretch
To the Nanga Parbat in the west, heft
The axe of temperatures, colder than cold.

Glacier to the west, glacier to the east,
In the mass of mist and snow, glaciers
Are, it seems, too loud and galore. Set to
Nature's peevish and cold command.

They are high and they are low, they
Have thin trees growing out of their navels,
Like the milk of paradise creating spots.
The mind is too strewn with them.

To the North is an outflow of glaciers.
Glued to the inland ice, sliding down an
Endless ablation, deposited at the Zemu,
Furious and fervish, debris of my soul.

Icy white Zemu, river of dark ice, retreat,
Then advance cheek by jowl, base of
Kanchenjunga, spirit of the song bird,
From the same corners, wither away ice.

Flanking its lateral moraine ridges
Zemu's innards are thin, like a sketch done
In no time, thinned out, year by year,
century by painful century, debris flooded.

The Khumbu glacier, wiser by the long
Years of quiet glory, older by the tall
Icefall unfazed by the diurnal course,
Iced, ice, and icier images, impaled.

Towered in by Khumbu, even death
Fears its icefall lurches, sagging under the
Weight of lusty climbers, stagger in lumps
Mountain deep, large crevasses tumble.

Warmed up, then cold again, Khumbu
Staggers in, crushing speed, crushing without
Warning, towers of ice move mercilessly,
Crunching, sternly denying even death wishes.

Large seracs collapse, without warning
Eluding its last definitions, as if mountains
Are the unkindest things of all, stern as death,
Collapse with a suddenness, intrigued.

Khumbu traps bodies as if they were wafers,
A billowing cloud of snow cleverly dusts itself,
Whispering winds, heavy blocks of ice, towers
Of billowing ice, moving, like shaking silence.

The dead sing where company comes,
Everest base camp a residue as Khumbu ice
Propels downward, rotating migrating, a force
Denied burial, as hearts laden with rue.

Compel fifteen thousand glaciers,
Small kingdoms by the reach of the eye
Their migration finds place in the rear
Of exposed crevasses, final meeting ground.

Another ice age, to every larger end
Another drop in glacier snowline
Turbid ardors of weather changing
Patterns, the remorseless deeps of time.

The Langtang glacier rolls round in
Preparative of its retreat, sensitive noise
Maker of new land, new clocks of change
In climates that plunge high, then low.

You, young Himalayan glaciers, sigh
Beating a retreat, corroded by a softer
Voice, still as new soil sites, new plants,
New over thrusts and faults, drive on.

The interglacial time of retreat has begun
Made brown with the edges of time, warm
As devotion, the global proclamation made,
Retreat, then advance, then retreat. Interwoven.

Dew locked Langtang beckons to Tibet,
Lands forlorn, as scrubby wedges driven,
Langshisa flows smooth through scrub land
And the tinsel wing between.

The feeble fluted peak mountain of
Gangchempo cut clever ridges of suspended
Symmetry, as the waters, herring scaled
The heavy surfaces of their silence.

Seventeen kilometers of curved and jagged
Highway of ice, Langtang leans northward,
And Langshisa glacier weeps as well, cold
And absolutely clear, as a yak's gaze.

And those five lakes, Panch Pokhari,
Holding hands together with the call
Of the red panda, lustrous eyes of our souls,
Their eyes gleam in the recesses, twined.

Jugal Himal has its remote perfumed air,
As the blue sheep, the bharal's gaze long
And far fronting the west, blooming horns,
Rutting, then return with elegance of spring.

Terrific as Tilman's Pass, cross
The heart with ropes and crampons
Glaciated regions of non native souls,
Horizontal spaced etchings spell death.

In the distant skies hangs Naya Kanga,
Southward flank of the alpine Langtang
Valley of lush ridges, blades of finesse,
What dread feet would climb its summit?

Gaze, gaze beyond the burning wonder,
The fiery peaks of Jugal Himal stare back,
Langshisa Ri seizes the moment, then the eyes
Turn higher toward Tibetan Shisapangma.

A grassy plain crests the tall ridges,
From where you watch, a long hum
Descends, the malty dregs mired,
Dead meat, dead animals keep her Shisha.

Age bent in human shape
Gosainkunda emerges, trapped within an
Eternal joy, when Shiva spat poison.
He feeds himself his own drink.

Searching for the sacred waters of
Immortality, the Gods churn them fast,
Then Shiva's throat turned blue, fearing
Demons, he drank, then spat.

Then thrust his trident into the grander
Grounds, as his rage resounds, so flows
Gosainkunda, sacred parchment of Shiva,
Submerged rocks, a bed of serpents seen.

So mountain mythologies are woven,
As shepherds quietly let the sheep graze,
Watch in an ecstasy of fumbling, then
Surpassed, toward a distant rest.

Bhutkunda sparkles, Nagkunda shines,
Dudhkunda too, and so does Surajkunda,
Through the thick blue green light of lakes
Bhairavakunda and Saraswatikunda sublime.

A vast deep delight of waters, a vast line of
Crystal waters, at the summit of mountains,
Their flashing eyes diamond like, their holy
Hair, secluded, like the weight of the Gods.

Far far away, the Annapurnas smile,
As if their creator rivalled a rigid God,
As if the pilgrim souls chanting annually
Make a blood poem of the whole.

They bring rice and flower offerings,
Their leaf platters pulled tight as they lug
Upward to Shiva's waters, their Hindu souls
Flicker, then divinely buoyant, brightening.

In the full moonlight of Janai Kerne
Holiness spits, by various arts of love,
Seeds of divine intensity, why bear the
Cordial fruit, why the choice in the embrace?

Loose rock mixed with snow, decline
Your head, full faced, in suit, beckons
The Ganja La crossing, sighing intimate,
A trail of fluttering flag free offerings.

Pressed against crevasses, pinched,
Craven to its glacial peak, Naya Kanga
Beckons its own propounded word,
Chimney shaped, snowed down.

The rock hard peaks of Kanshuram,
Urkinmang and Ganchenpo, blow
Words of sacred love, a blessed ghost,
Sending gentle sleep from blue heaven.

Of an old lama, Dorjee, and of his wife
Lakpa, and of their ox running up the river,
Into the Langtang valley, until the chase
Took away the ox's life, with breathless tools.

Walk in fear and dread, walk over the
Holy ground of an ox hacked to death,
Walk over the large flat rock, red moss
And lichen tossed, licking its own blood.

Its magic marks unfurl the Lantang Ri
Across the banks of the upper Trisuli,
Wear out with its own running, past Rasuwa
Hallowed, new emblems born, of Dorjee Lakpa.

More than fifteen thousand glaciers form
An envious sight, almost a third pole;
All of them consented, in grace and feature,
The frozen locks of tall snow line.

Higher than the highest, like pearls apart,
No space to breathe within, permanent snow line,
Like crystal shining armor, always snowed in,
Strapped to those jewels, tightened ever.

Siachin, a shining orb of a glacier,
Your eastern Karakoram range keeps it
Safe, interposed in glacier like ease,
Northeast, in cold yet cheerful logic.

Long, long as the sighs of wrecked soldiers,
Forty seven miles of untampered ice, plunging
Down to sea level, like dodged icy sprite, then
Rise, sucking the blood of those fighting.

In vainglory, defined by nations that draw
Their breath in; Far along the war drums sounding
Line of control that rebukes Siachin's simple
Chasmed fears, long, long betrayed.

Deliberately named, deliberate abundance
Of roses, Siachin sings its paeans of derision,
Such gorging of pure ice, such a red vision
Of roses growing in suspended transport.

South of an imponderable watershed,
Siachin is a dim white smudge, separating
The grand debate within the Eurasian plate,
Locked within a tussle, one country, now split.

Bestrides the icy fights, the last steps
Of soldiers are heard, cold and cheerful,
Whistling loudly between the Saltoro Ridge
And the Karakoram to the bitter east.

With ice that refuses to trickle down,
From the Sia Kangri peaks that seem to
Settle forever, ingrained like an eternal
Photograph, the Saltoro ridge shines.

Its steep crest hears the heavens filled
With shouting, a peace that is forever,
Lasting through the wilderness aboard
Crude, brood in the deep ice.

Through the deep passes on the ridge,
Sia La, Bilafond La, Yarma La, Gyong La,
Yulung La, pass by with a white veil,
Heavens so clear, blind the sun's light.

Amid this majestic vista of coldness,
Amid the unhurrying chase of more ice,
Siachin needs be gobbled up by the politics
Of imagination, betray me or betray thee.

Dotted lines that shed a heavier shadow
Than falls from the night of control,
Cease fires that blind the sun's lights, NJ982,
Of woe and war on sad and angry lands.

At the dawn of birth, two nations divided
By errors of cartography, by the dark earth,
By the storms of a spent rage, kneeling, keeling,
A silence implying so much.

Such fate falls upon demarcations,
Entreating chastity for more of itself, as if
Maps are the hands of gods, the sunrise
Opening on human wills so far gone.

Why would you care for human glory
Being so glorious in yourself, unflawed
And so clear? Why would military outposts
Rise and ring and spoil the unspoiled?

Incursions spring only from the dark
Depths of human rage. To make you
The highest battleground, filled and
Flooded, as silence surging backward.

Like a fount, explosive and then dull,
Why mark you with obscure mists, those
Dull shards of intermittent fighting
Hate hangings amid your peace?

Your praise faded, peddled on
The murky stage of human blood
The lark's note disturbed, outposts
Of mortal folly, storm-clothed.

Why would you nurse a wound, a
Military presence in your exalted armor,
Those broad shoulders of a sublime
Song cry about the high costs of war?

If sacredness is a garment, you wear it,
You do not need peace parks of sorts
Like running water that freezes, killed by your
Unforgiving cold, Kargils freeze, disengage.

TWO

REFLECTING

Like strips of you, the majesty of the Himalayas,
Like a child from your womb, your rivers and lakes,
Like multi lettered, many meaning, one syllabled word,
Demand reverence, a space filled with your own being.

The five sisters make, a wish for keen deflection,
Vitasta, Askini, Irawati, Vipasha, and Shatadru flow,
Through ancient channels, changing names. Indus,
Brahmaputra, Ganga, Yamuna and Spiti, float by you.

All sidelong bending, making space through
Your steep armor. Blowing a whistle, of watery blue
In your stillness, fill your heart with their waters, as
Your power expands, enriched, in harmony.

Jhelum river now, Vitasta as Shiva dug a spear
A measure of his thumb and finger, forking out
Parvati, the evidence of his triumph; call upon her,
Evoke a river from the nether world.

Affirm the conception of a river, a Sapta Sindhu,
A God born in beauty, in power, and in goodness,
Slither west between two countries, now parted,
Heroic conception of Verinag spring, the melodist.

Its praise increased by the Greeks of yore,
When Alexander cast a shadow on Porus,
Put centuries beside the Jhelum river; cast
A pall of gloom, what purpose gave him victory.

Chenab too sings to the glory of the Jhelum,
Rivers that cut through discord, as the choir
Of the waters outsings, the quiet beauty of Srinagar;
Wide eyed, lustily, swiftly flowing brown waters.

With a scraping squeal, the Verinag spring
Births the river, then a mute observance hangs;
An octagon reassumes itself on a circular base,
Sourcing the Jhelum, and the tall pine trees gush.

Surrounding them both, gazing mysteriously,
The Pir Panjal looks down at the broad river,
Sighing through its feet, clinging and spreading,
Its feeble uproar ripples through its shoulders.

The Kashmir valley tickles, in slow caresses,
Even Wular lake feels, its deep languors, as
Marbled clouds scud by, so does Jhelum; then
Enters languages alien, through a deep gorge.

It finds its roots of sweet relish, the sweet
Moans of Neelum and Kunhar, its tributaries,
The Jhelum has been taught to cover gently,
As the heavier shadows fall, its lusty lungs.

Contained within; through ruddy orchards
Of the doab, the welter of the parching wind;
Confluences sweet, now merge with the Chenab,
The underwater tensions, the compressed silt.

Ah Chenab! Your body still gleams like gold,
Askini, the moon still watches you, as you murmur
Words bitten off the matter of a smile, the charm
Of your riverlike smile, gilden, sharp.

Through the upper reaches of your mountains,
downed with muddy blue light, the Chenab rises,
With sleep and icy darkness all around, in patterns
Of snow melting, leaning out, in melodious tear.

At Bara Lacha Pass, the Chandra and the Bhaga,
Rivers dreaming of mountain peace, their trembling
Hands conjoin, with mock patience, as Chandrbhaga.
Magnified sounds, of rural ease, nursing together.

The voice of one song, the Chandrabhaga sports
With the Marau, as the thrush and the robin sing,
One song, across many mountains, with one light,
Become the Chenab, the bright drench of one river.

Through the blinding heart of consciousness,
Intrinsic myth secured, the summer songs chime,
Through layered centuries of time, the Chenab
Entwines, in single crystals, devoutly bind.

Six hundred miles of river-throated song,
Through Jammu and the Punjab, sustained
Sounds of beatitude, embrace the Jhelum,
And the Sutlej, swinging together, as Panjnad.

Five rivers flow through ripe fields, iridescent,
Upborne by the soft silk of water, the fair lips,
Knitted together in the webbing, one shady brow
Bounded over by your mountains, deep set glory.

The Ravi has eyes bright as light, Irawati
Coils and bursts out, gyrating like a Himalayan
River, north westerly prismatic blue blood coursing,
Through its north westerly veins, grasped.

Wilting in the arms of your glacial fields, mid
Himalayan beauty sprung in the throes of
Boulders, massed horns of twisted memories,
Breathless, point to point, shattered river bed.

Pressing through river gorge of fire,
Creeping closer, rapid that roll into one
Another's arms, the process of a deep glare,
Walk, then range through Kangra, spasmodic gait.

Ravi's Himachal beauty is transbound,
With narrow forehead, then ringing grooves,
Feeding off snow melt, ample warrant
Of writhing pools of rapids, gorgeous white.

The Budhil and Nai flash lightning strong,
Branching Ravi into winged tributaries, over heath
And dale, over valley and forest, sacred as life,
Coming back to the proceeds of Chamba valley.

Ravi trapezes down the hills of Dalhousie, breathing
Hard with the restless winds on the hill sides, its
Terraced fields filled with the zest of sprouting,
Its inlets stare, stark beauty of green valleys.

Ravi can attack with full fury, tissue preserved,
Gather with earnestness full blown, sturdy trees,
Move westward over the Dhauladhar range, then
Twist and move its eyes south, carry it along.

Your Himalayan slopes and valleys shed your
Skin, as eminent but freak catchments, wax,
The Bhadal, Siul, Baira, Ujh, and Tant Gari,
Smooth your rough touches, tributary wise.

And the Beas river, like a rolling phrase,
Just another that tests your Himalayan might,
Amid your towering crests in Himachal, Vipasha
Aka Beas rises, swiftly, from breast of Rohtang Pass.

The Beas, riddled with myths, of a drowning
Sage, Vyasa, saved by your power, the gushing river,
Enhances your grandeur, like pride in the breasts
Of the starry pavilion, jewels elementing it.

With the drunk delight of battles vanquished,
Beas flows from Kullu to Mandi to Kangra, in
Thunderous conflict, fading gleams of sharp
Curves, challenging its own northern flight.

Just as you darken the world around you,
Just as Alexander's dreams dissolved, gleaming
In the maelstorm of defeat, just as the Beas witnessed
His broken heart, just so, flowing along, unbroken.

Beas marshaled, its outer face nudged
In the pillow of unstable peace, in a lighter
Tread, in the order of ancient battles, its
Meaning undivined, lost, slept away.

Marked by mildness of temper, the Beas
Twists and turns, three hundred miles of
Sopping wet life, then merge with the Sutlej,
Dissevered your wings from its blue shoulders.

Prodigious as the Vyasa Kund, the birthmark
Of a humming hive, a river of dreams, so do its
Tributaries, Awa, Bain, Luni, Banganga, Uhal,
Scatter the measured song, the touch, a watery hand.

The Sutlej, or Shatadru of ancient times,
Rising from Langa lake in a menacing long
Journey through your Himalayan bones;
Nor crushed by it, marshaled in order.

Of a nine hundred mile long battle,
Harvested, winged on the shoulders of
Deep gorges, rooted in South west Tibet,
Almost burning the cavernous breasts.

Bleared and smeared by your smudged
Surface, Sutlej flows west, reflecting your
Snows; Red river of your milk white dreams,
Unwearied still, flowing, keeping time.

North of the Vindyas, hills like shaggy Shoulders,
Sutlej flows by the mercy of
Your tectonic visions, the clouds above
You enfold, mythical ashes of the Saraswati.

And still in the quiet wonders of your
Crimson gold, cracking through the guts of
Your Hindukush ranges, the Sutlej deduces
Particular memories of your soul.

Refulgent as the dome above, a crown
Of quick perspective, the Sutlej meanders,
Through valleys gilt with green gold,
Through the Tibetan Shipki La Pass.

Twisting and turning through your
Nebulous ways, through the sleeping
Earth of time, the Sutlej meets the Beas,
Your Himachal hills, so tall with prophecy.

Stretching afar, in the upper reaches of
A Tibetan time, hung still, in gradients
Of gold, the Sutlej valley, a Garuda center,
Of Zhangzang, lost on the horizon.

Your Himalayan rains descend, drowning
The Sutlej with strange shapes, like restless
Armies of soldiers, the waters rising, like
Lofty rhyme, like a destined urn, overgrown.

And still another one, the Indus serpents
Forth, under the opening eyelids of a lake,
Mansarovar sleeps amid your hoary, haze
Cradled mountains, a far different scene.

In the ever wintry Tibetan plateau, the
Indus is born, its soul doing its benumbing
Rounds, gushing through Ladakh, its healing,
Long southerly, far and dissociate, Sindhu.

Feeding off your glaciers, the Indus flows
Through Vedic times, ancient river over wasted
Lands, pursuing the quest of the curious, with
Larger faith, large as the tidal bore.

What is grandeur to Indus, carving and curling,
When it is nulled by the river's glacial powers?
At the meeting ground of Sengge and Gar,
Flattened by the ghost quick, living waters.

Your mountain ranges soar above, braided,
Nganglong Kangri and Gang Rinpoche stare,
Fixed gaze, eagle eyes, sternly, a dark flush
From the west, and the Indus flows on, northwest.

Looking down, you form a quick parabola,
Entering against massive gorges, against the
Force of water, turn around, then move westward,
A circle swoop, a slow girdle unfurled, push, push.

The lion's mouth is a mothering source, a twitch,
Mount Kailash turns upon itself, such a water loop,
Sacred mountain, sacred mother of rivers, sacred form,
Propped on, lofty bough of strength, trembling hand.

Brahmaputra, casting its crown of blue and
Gold, a timid creeping out of Angsi glacier,
A river of gold surges out, and your mountains
Reverberate through Tibet, a vast expanse.

Yarlung Tsangpo, a river, its visionary brow
In Tibet, Brahmaputra unlocks its male heart,
Carving volatile canyons of colored waters,
A thrill of waves, serpentine, egotistical.

While the winds run low from field to field,
While Brahmaputra meanders, through gorges
That never went amiss, storming and clouding,
The skies widen, gleam, then tender ashen.

Changing names, like envelopes, now Siang,
Or Dihang, flowing into Arunachal; then like a
Gilded cable, through Assam; stir all the birds
Awake in Bangla country, flood the earth there.

Brahmaputra, this river of cleaving wing,
An intimate welding of small channels, weave
Through each other's hearts, network of teeming
Water, braided, refined, cool rooted splits, rejoined.

Three thousand miles of coursing, through
Channels, abandoned, formed anew, fluttering
Among new channels, novel islands, buffeted by
The hungry breath of water basins, roused up.

Racing, now damming, the Brahmaputra heaves
Its waters like furniture, pale loiterings, nodding
Arms, unstable river banks suggest something, then
The Jamuna pops its head into the Bay of Bengal.

Now, the Ganga takes off from your blinding
Bright glacier; the mouth of a cow widens itself
To a dazzling belt, then narrow, then sublime,
An immortal journey starts from your raw sinews.

As the winds blow from one mountain to another,
As snakes spinning through your Uttarakhand peaks,
So do the Bhagirathi, Alaknanda, Mandakini, Pindar,
And the Dhauliganga breed their headstreams, sacred.

Your Nanda Devi peak unravels, anxiously
Lies awake, as Alaknanda unweaves northward,
Breaking free of parental constraints, the Satopanth
And the Bhagirath Kharak glaciers, ice birthing.

Singing songs of the trinity, the Satopanth lake
Trembles to the lore of Brahma, Vishnu, and Shiva,
At the Satopanth glacier's snout, Alaknanda river
Speaks the tongue of Gods, ripening to the core.

Such a town as Badrinath, your harness jingles
On the banks of the Alaknanda, the birds find it
Hard to stir awake, to fly around the Nar and Narayan;
Peaks that stay unaroused, drugging memories.

A scattered chapter awakens, the roar of the
Bhagirathi flows with scalding unguents,
A subglacial meltwater cave adorns, the river's
Heart lies where Gangotri soared. Ejected.

In headstreams that unite, where the waters
Of Alaknanda and Bhagirathi touch, where rain
And pain collide, there Ganga emerges, cutting,
Riddling your Himalayan sides. From your cradle.

Past the Siwalik mountain range, from the
Depth of heaven above, from the cleavage of
The outer Himalayas, unsheafing, those beauteous
Locks of Shiva, are like nymphs unbounded.

Yamuna or Jumna, tributary of the Ganga,
Draws off silence, rising from your great Himalayan
Slopes, a blue garment from the Banderpunch
Massif, leaving a tender ashy river glow.

Flow in a poised leap, gentle as pearls
Push in a southerly direction through your
Kingly feet, play around the green and neutral
Tints of your Himalayan rich foothills, streaking.

Then dazzle into an exiting belt, spread along
The binding hills of Uttarakhand, span the horizons
Onto the Gangetic plains. Each advancing step on
The Doab, a bringer of new waters, sacred.

The Yamuna gleams with colored light, while
Earth lifts its sacredness. The Yumnotri glacier
Birthing a river spun between a sun god for
A father, full points of light, zenithward.

To keep at divine beauty, securely bright,
Its rims of blue shaped by Yami, quick waves
Of death, stooping sister of Yama, mighty in
Death, intact in its agitations, propelled.

Glorious as Yamuna, as the sparks fly upward,
Taking a dip in its waters, neither mist nor shade
A beatitude felt, locked in by its waters,
River born of your breath, a purple glow.

A river that disguises our fears, symmetrically
Pointed, as being released from the torments,
Of Death and of dying, like a blind man's dream;
Music showers their upturned faces, soak it in.

And yet another river, Spiti, faces a glacial
Distance, between plump and barren mountains;
Locked into your Kunzum range, unstrung,
Water drains Pin valley, gathered radiance.

The green dazed intelligence of the Spiti valley,
Its soul playing between Tibet and India, land lying
Suspended, stretched at the cross roads, middle land,
Amid desert mountains that compel, subtle effluence.

Daring as never before, the Lahaul and Spiti wrap,
Your high mountain ranges; a solemn mortician cuts
At the Rohtang Pass, ice burying the Kunzum,
And more snow comes like a selfless forager.

As if to keep design from spilling into a
Spectacle of intense beauty, as if to withdraw
From the lovely southwesterly winds, Spiti bursts
With rain water, steering its broad satin banks.

Circumference of bold mountains, hefty with
The soul and flesh of Buddhist thoughts; the
Enduring nature of cultural arts bear fruit,
Humming hive of thriving Tibetan markets.

The stretched hands of Spiti river, the
Stretched soul, spurt into Kabzian and
Teopo streams; dive down northerly paths,
From Manali to Kaza, a thunder of liquid.

As if the earth is her ornament, as if
It is splendor to descend east to Kaurik; then
Meet the Sutlej, with the sun in his heaven,
Settling a deep intense color in itself.

As if descended from the honey dew
Of glacier symphony, Spiti river weaves
A circle along the monasteries, full echoing
Its music loud and long; spiritual peace.

Close your eyes to feel her flowing hair,
The Buchen Lamas drunk in the milk of
Paradise, look into the grey eyes of villages,
Golden sheaves, the calm of Ki monastery.

THREE

SNOWING

Come unto me, whispers Mount Everest;
Sagarmatha, as the Nepalese strain strums
The upward path is one kind of good bye, Tibetan
Chomolungma, is Earth's highest mountain.

The sweet spirits of your mountains, repeat:
Come unto me, the voice of the Gods unfold,
In Mount Everest, twenty nine thousand feet high,
Shine in the holy glimmer, in Mahalangur Himal.

Mount Everest stands, with graceful intellection,
Deep beneath its mind, cut by faults and flexures;
Silence, standing there, with Lhotse, Nuptse,
and Changtse, capture its glances. Supreme.

Clouds and storms pass you by, so what if
Your name has an English sense of stealing?
A wayfaring traveler outsings, crumbling
Ice chunks that dislodge, down labyrinthine

Ways. Those steep clefts down the throat
Of Mount Everest, the North Face turns the
Blood cold, alpine style, a creased map of
Sullen ridges, no dwelling place in death zone.

South Col does betray, nature's privileges
Halt. Between the sharp edged notches, what
Is perceived, dies, neither evil thoughts nor ice
Rest on this death zone; no rest nor pass between.

The Yak route, its amassed patterns of Sherpa,
Sacred amid the supreme solitude, guiding angels,
Within the winding ways of specter thin thread,
Of life, of sleep, of food that is overwrought.

The upward path unwearied, as sherpas cook;
Shake the frail ridging; porters who climb the
Ever fixed mark, the tear blinded horn;
Else fall down the wizard roar of death.

Else chart an approach through, low depths
Of a snow ridge, the bite of glaciers turns
Corpses green. In the raging calm of the
North Col, beyond the illusion of a ridge.

And ever as the Holy Mother Peak,
Waxes, then shifts, plate tectonics becomes
An approved art, detachments, reluctant,
Low angle faults, the chant, unheard, unsung.

Rocks that contain untraced faults,
Rocks that sediment the hymns of time,
Rocks that metamorphose, forms of
Lingering notes, only a moss grows.

Like a toothy horned grimace, injected,
Those narrow walls of high speed winds,
A loud, sound splitting bassoon, fast and
Freezing jet stream, not even furtive pity.

Injected into the stratosphere, in a
Long white gown, confused, mounted and
Dressed in snow, blizzards that spew an
Unremembered time, and avalanches

That could freeze death in its path,
The turbid ardor of its rumbling, a thick
Blast of rock, ice and wind sliding, gliding,
Then shudder through its own massed head.

The Khumbu icefall shakes, a vision of
Icy carnage. Down Mount Pumori, deeply
Confused by its own daring, the salt of its
Imaginings unimagined, unsalted wrath.

Sagarmatha, frozen forehead of the sky,
Who would emulate you, pulling off your
White colors against the roof, Mount Everest,
The holy hush of a Goddess Mother descends.

And K2, the second highest, nods in its cone.
Savage Mountain, battles the unsure extinction
Of human hope. Unfamiliar Karakorum monster,
The Baltoro glacier weeps, birthing K2.

Flush from its rancor, the snow clad steep sides
Tempestuous sheath overspread, K2 carries
The fate of its climbers, coarsely patched,
Rumble, draw your last breath on its wild temper.

Kanchenjunga peak, grandeur rises between Nepal
And Sikkim, reclines its snowy head. Stagnated
Within a curtain of sheer clouds, straight topped.
Gazing hand in hand, with the holy monarchs.

Your majestic Kanchenjunga peak nearly
Fulfills a promise, stay inviolate, nor touch your
Honor blooming around your head. A polished
Post spilling loudly from its bare spots.

Countenance divine, filled with fine five
Treasures, silver and gold, gems that glow
With a million treasured, religious texts pursued
With a hard hand, and food grains, a holy hush.

Five peaks, whose triumph rings with a
Brassy sound; end stopped between the Tamur
River and the Teesta. Whisper a little tenderness,
As we offer our greetings to the fulsome five.

Like white arms, braceleted and enduring
Nature's girdled mountain massif, to view
Your living frame, strangely glorious heights,
And heaps of ice divine, beat your wide wings.

Glacier, glacier everywhere; the lofty Zemu
Glacier to the northeast; proud Talung glacier casts
Southeast glances; Yalung glacier spreads
Southwestward; Kangchen, propelled northwest.

And another set of massif, Nanda Devi,
As if peaks were museum pieces, as if
Uttarakhand ripens the earth, bursting glory,
A glacial basin, an icy ring of peaks.

As in a bucketful of snow, drip by
Drip, Nanda Devi, hardened by its own
Snow; a flight of uncarpeted angled steps,
Through a mist, thoroughly vapor kissed.

The falsetto in the raw throat of Rishi
Ganga, the old subject of a defile; like
The poles and broken spires of a white world,
As Nanda Devi Park divines a chasm.

Like women running away from pleasure,
So in its plashless glaciers, the southern
And the northern Rishi glaciers sit stern;
And Rishi Ganga flows up and down, rent

A bit through steep ridges, like the whim of
Death, between flame and iron, caught
Between Ramani glacier and Trishul, like
The strong eyes of a goddess, divine, knowing.

Song sung by Gori Ganga, bliss giving.
The alpine meadows gathered, of lovely
Worth, pristine as birth, harsh as the birthing
Of its rimmed summits, a Garhwal Himalayan

A veil embraces a fortress, its touch, sublime.
Sacred as Goddess Parvati Mother. Daughter of
Hills, across the silent face of Lord Shiva, Nanda
Devi, consort, blameless, goodness extreme.

Twinned messengers of goodness, who can
Say what shape or form? Parvati or Durga,
Rock or ice, rage or benevolence, Nanda Devi
Heralds the grand debate within shrines.

Hardeol, poised above, undraws the curtain
To the Temple of God, climbing over,
Thinking of rightness, its metaphysics
As the Kumaon Himalayas explode, inland.

A glittering in the veins of Ikalari,
Glacier all still and stiff, explain its
Eastern approach, to the Hardeol icefall,
Fat pockets of cold, south of Milam valley.

When Hardeol peak shows, an underwater
Flash, abandon all the guardian angels
Of Nanda Devi, come with whirling feet,
Up the Trishuli valley, and Munsiyari gleams.

Brimming with light, Trishul peak,
Is shot with silver trident light, almost as if
Shiva oozes through the Kumaon, his pale
Lamps lit, his splendours, speak nothing.

In these mountains, in Rishiganga valley,
There is no shadow, only the sparkle,
Only the touchstone quietness of
Trishul glacier, amid the evening glow.

If the four peaks of Chaukhamba could
Stir, the sun would wheel by in its
Gangotri reflections, like the splayed
Tongues of four pillars, a Shivling.

It holds a perpetual throne, a maze
Of boulders, the Gangotri glacier
Throws off its icy clasp, then Nilakanth
Looms large in the horizon, retreat.

From the Garhwal Himalayan bed,
Chaukhamba make a warm display,
An outside chance, its unbroken pride,
Alaknanda river rises from the base.

Lhotse peak brings its own tidings, a
Hushed silence, a Tibetan conjoining,
South face of the lofty Everest, and the
Blank cold skies, staring within.

A glacial blue ice, Lhotse peaks, then
Bulges, then connects to Everest, overrun
A long crest and South Col, peaks continue
-Ing, in vertical ridges, withdrawn.

Lonesome bindings. Still in continuum
With Nuptse peak, a cold strong mass
Between China and Nepal, a west peak
Resting in ill placed conjoined glory.

Seven peaks fused in one, detached,
Compounds strange, a stern and massive
Sense of passivity. Repository of your
Stone faced Himalayan dreams.

Kamet peak too seems to sleep, topped
By golden dreams, all severing rise amid
The Garhwal Himalayas, a giant pyramid,
Flat topped, rearranging two peaks, almost.

In the Zaskar mountains, misaligned fragments
Of time sweep in, a strange disappearing,
Brush, as the cold winds rush in, rocks seem to
Catch impassive fire; the Tibetan plateau dazed.

Catch the shivers, mount rock walls,
Kamet dulls, then shines with glacial light, its
Steep gulleys wobble with pain, denied
The power of fear, succumb to winds, head bowed.

The snows lie steep on Kamet, its soul
Detached, dread amid cratered valleys,
Mukut, Mana, Bidhan, Deoban, whisper,
Abi Gamin, look askance, peaks surround.

When Ganesha's tusk moves in Mana,
Epics get written, at sunset when Ved Vyasa
Watched, the unbroken glory of your sunsets,
Then do divine ghosts move.

Or it may be a fit haven for
Saltoro Kangri as it leans, like a fluted
Ladakhi steeple, Saltoro Kangri summits,
Then descends into oropolitical divisions.

The fragile gates of Siachin defy,
Those exhausting, glaciated ridges burn
Closed in, edged leafpoints, curled in feet of
Blizzards, again the Siachin glacier survives.

Avalanches that rip the edges of life,
Like a gilded shell, the turning tide of
Siachin swells, a haughty attitude, man eating
Crevasses that punch, pinched.

Saser Kangri peak nibbles, five brothers
That spew the profound wisdom, huddle
Around Kashmir, tread in austere ways,
Reach toward Shukpa Kunchnag glacier.

Beneath the rippled pulses of the Nubra,
Beneath the eerie oblivion of Sakang,
And Chamshen glaciers, resounds,
Cordial notes of western Nubra valley.

Circulate over the bright edges,
The Shyok river bends sharply,
Then looks upward in stunned gaze,
Saser Kangri looks down, isolated.

And in magnificent stillness, stands
Mamostang Kangri peak, far from the
Blinding sight, the remote Ladakhi reaches,
Quietened, stricken, where no birds sing.

The cold winds shift around Thangman,
Broken glacier of broken dreams. The open
Crevasses become spinning tops; gradients
That spellbind, jagged peaks, look down.

Mamostong, South Terong, and South
Chong Kumdan glaciers, birth deeper
Lights, deeper snows; rugged Ladakh
Sways, with full swung breasts.

A dense fog surrounds five ridges,
Mamostang rests within; a thousand
grandeurs, its conical shape, healing,
The concentric rigor of medicine.

Forbidden terrain of forbidden dreams
Gorges, high passes, flat valleys,
Through gorges, where all twists and turns,
Fast flowing rivers, all interiorized.

Desolate, complex folds of full towering
Peaks, Rimo Muztagh, Siachen Mustagh,
Saser Muztagh, the intricate connections of
Undiminished, tall things.

The Rimo massif goes down,
Like a faded paper sheet in Karakorum;
Full striped mountain peak, your late
Siachin birthings, like wrinkled peas.

The Rimo look of striated time, glaciated,
The Shyok river arches only when its clinched
Fist, deeply gorged, opens at its wide basin.
And the snout of the Rimo glacier, flickers.

Fingers full of precious gems, Mount Kailash
Glows with crystal, ruby, gold, and lapis lazuli,
Ruling at its azure heights, Shiva sits in peace
Extraordinary, yogic peace, undispersed.

Precious jewel of the illustrious, who placed
You, Mount Kailash, near the blue burst of
Lake Mansarovar, at the edge of this earth,
Paving a path toward the skies, heaven ward.

What does a walk around the mountain do?
Why circle the invincible jade lake?
I am the symbol, I am the Shakti,
Echoes the great mountain.

FOUR

INHABITING

Will the snow birds sing an ode,
To the dandelions and the mountain sorrel,
The soil beneath that sustains, then break
Into the trailing streams and lakes?

Through the verdant gorges that
Tumble down, the densely tufted
Rhododendrons sparkle in the sun, pay
Themselves off as ecosystem engineers.

Acidify the mountain soil, their
Wonted impulses give in, else benefit
Themselves, like the gusts swelling,
Threatened, corpse like, unseeded.

Amid the western alpine shrub land,
Amid the rumbling voices, rhododendrons
Fuse with the voices of summer, the cold
On a long wet Himalayan leash.

The moss hanging on Chir pines, giant
Leaps of dirges singing, the alpine
Zones awaken, the thin hanging conifers
Spin their ovoid cones in languor.

Their red brown barks startle at
The stillness, the fissured trunk
Withstand centuries of your weight,
The needle leaves spread outward.

Pines beguile the eastern stretches,
White pines, blue pines, Chilgoza pine,
Let fall upon their back, those western
Outposts, lowlands of your firmness.

Among them clogging, taller conifers
The Deodar cedars with their fixed eyes,
Long arms, needle long, seemingly random
Shooting through your western pits, star like.

Their barrel shaped cones, filled with
Antique female intensity, tremble to
Despoil themselves, their winged seeds
Look back on you with true kind eyes.

Deodar, wood of the gods, joyful
As the light in the eyes of sages
Glory be to Shiva, their sorrows
Dimmed, in the candlelight of their dreams.

Incense of your indwelling, aromatic
As the horizontal spread of branches,
Pubescent, bidding speed to stateliness,
Droop downward, medicinal end.

Temperate on the edge of doom
As the mixed conifers, evergreen forests
Murmur by the western hour, along the
Sutlej and the Ganges, rivers without rest.

Weep, weep like the spruce trees,
Or wipe them with your thin needles,
Flapping in pendulous branchlets,
Spruces, drugged, every atom of them.

Those western Morindas have their homes
In decorative circles of souls, whose glass is
Run, suddenly mounted in ornaments, a green
Brilliance tempered with a droop.

And so would your glory be blasted without
The great western fir? Lofty as sunrise without
Its brimming edges, ornamentally jump start
Your threaded dance through those silver underparts.

Separated leaves confer a power, a luminous
Cloud of conifers overspread with phantom hue,
Like a silver thread woven through it,
Like a silvery silver, daring, floating.

Dry, dry, dry. If dryness is an outlet for death,
Passing through the green speared mist of
Broad leafed forests, dry winds sing with
Mournful voices, or dreaded martyrdom.

But the oaks stay resilient, dryness only a
Balm to their big bodied delicious selves,
They ape life in giving life. Firewood and tools,
Hand along collateral leaves for nutrients.

They ask for nothing, useless and free,
Oaks stand dour and dark, biotic stress beginning
A history of dried up grief, Oh whither, the hardy
Oak, the trusty oak, flattened logs of life.

White oak, brown oak, green oak,
Against a community of twistings, treeline
Mingle with lichen and with fungi,
Walking over them, unseen.

Acorns gone, thinning shadows, nodes,
Catkins on the banj oaks, wrinkled,
Hollow heads of tortured glory,
Low hanging, distended, stressed.

Straggling dull leaves, stiff with
Invisible troubles, leathery, estranging,
Sharp teeth on the edges, unplumbed
Wired branches, secluded recesses.

The banj oaks only observe the honor
And grace, drowsing off on earth made
Old by shale and limestone, the essence
Of geology, stem end and slow roots

Stuck amid mica shist, gneiss,
And quartzite, flecks of their past
Showing through. Their people-ness
Defined in Kumaun style, magnified.

By their simplicity, saved by a
Lowness that will flame out with freshness.
Thinned by a splinter. Singing in style,
In rainy autumn days, gorgeously.

But the lords of the higher areas, the
Kharsu oaks that hold their breath,
Surviving in heavenly hurt, high above,
Wear the green wedding garments high

Above at the highest elevation,
In quest of higher miracles perhaps,
Stepping outward, the geological
formations that support their flashing lights.

Wide eyed, the best of people's trees,
Tilonj oaks lean and look over the wetness,
Thrive on mesic gossamer ground,
With dews that quiver and thrill, loving.

They avoid dryness, tossed down,
Strapped and sprinkled, their resurrection
Defined by higher roots, moistured by
The last syllable of magic.

Turning away from the shady spots.
Rianj oaks reveal, a mannerly devotion,
Surviving on sunny slopes, they pray,
Grant virtues to the flight of the sun.

Noiseless dwellers of the Himalayas,
Oaks are oaks, firm, uncomplaining,
The good increase of sandy, loamy soils,
When the winds stop, when the worms devour.

And you still survive, along with the dwarf
Himalayan junipers, bruised by their own
Sweetness, practicing all their compact charm,
Drooping, spreading, exacerbated shrub of all.

Junipers are mystical; Junipers are the dark green
Matter of mountains, Dhupi women of the skies,
Kissing in an immeasurably high way, long and
Mysterious, cool and sweet, Khadros.

Burn them, burn the junipers, stir up
Fragrances, tablets of divine bubbling,
Purify and sanctify, casements of unhistoric
Rituals, dissevered sky dwellers.

Coniferously coned, your mouths open
Magnifying your sky doors. Descend the ladder
Of starry smoke, cleanse all, like angels in heaven,
Energize, the clear vowels of disinfectants.

Juniper oil, poking and stirring, apparently
Distilled by smiling poems, another page of
Physical revival, the spirit touched too,
Whitewashed, spread long trailing branches.

And the lush valleys support hemlocks,
Tall as your bones, with ovoid crowns,
Spires of single piece, pendulous bushes
A bravado that boasts ornamental age.

The old hemlocks repay themselves.
Multiple stems spring out, pyramidic
Irregularities, grey brown, showtunes
That shake, shallow, sinuous boles.

Under starry nights, their spiral leaves
Anchored in original horizontal veins,
Tales of their glory and grain, their open
Ends, rounded and obtuse. Sunken

Midribs bent in strange fashions, devour
Their silvery stomatal bands, curved down
Thin winged flowers burst in dreams that
Ask odd questions, stop the earth.

With seeds that slip betimes away, coned
Purely by chance, globose and sacs wide
Grasped firmly from the tops of your
Himalayan longings of the heart.

And in the loftier light of your western
Mountains, maples grow with summon calls
That form a thin roof. Quaintly neat
But brighter than green gems.

For their startling beauty, piteously
Grand maples, a watershed protection,
Like clanged bars. Seeds that mature
Untroubled by the golden gateway of stars.

That stare down at clumps of aesculus,
Alder, poplar, birch and willows, thrive
With an instancy near streams. Then drop
Their odors beyond the rise.

When darkness sets into those
broad leaved forests, as music round
the shell of their barks, their wetness
chants for peace, fortress of hope.

As age upon age dawns, as orchids
Bloom amid the heavier shadow, the
Woe and war of creepers descends, mingle
Evergreens, the grimace of deciduous trees.

For something sufficiently varnished dry,
Gather the stacks upon your low foothills,
Within the simmering range of summer,
Marked with evergreen shining leaves.

True to their charge, wild pomegranates
Come to light, with dreams of being
Far removed from the luminous cloud,
Live to reap the ripened earth for a century.

And time's flow brightens your western
Mountains with oleanders. Desert roses,
Crinkled with the fresh dews of night, as
Their nectar gives medicinal hope.

Turbid ardors drape their silky tendrils,
Oleanders share the pomp inlooped
In their broad crinkled leaves, pink and red,
Give, give, then fade in your glimmering cliffs.

And olives too strike root with
Their overtaking wings, plunging through
The wilder heart of your existence,
Reaping harvests in fearless flames.

Ranging through the low foothills,
With blinded eyesight under the sere
And hot suns, the olives and the oleanders
Overspread, as a carpet, breathing joy.

Viewing the games of love they are
Capable of, the evergreen laburnum
Lifts its own sweet being in distinctive
Display of bright sunny colors.

The laburnum's heart wears wings
Its evergreen person makes a rapturous
Greeting to the juices of the earth, even
As it never self-destructs its own tenderness.

Rounded shapes sprout furry buds
Impatiently anoint their destiny in bright
Yellow legume flowers, as thin silk
Spikes, their vanilla smelling blood lingers.

Puget blue or Zanzibar yellow, your
Hungry heart finds protection against fences
And walls, where the margins fade,
The broad foundations of laburnum hope.

In the lower regions of your sensuous and
Warm patches, the Indian gooseberry also grows,
Like an umbrella of amla beads, let loose from
A broken necklace, where your heart stirs.

So much wealth to be hatched there,
There is only so much, the intuitive
Will realize, only so many discover
Nuggets of vitaminic unlatchings.

And the Sal trees grow there as well,
Offer so much, unfurl tender mysteries,
The Sal leathery leaves float upward, scatter
Comforts even for a Buddha, close the cycle.

Nodding their yellow flowers, only a bare
Echo from the land of early laurelled crowns,
On tough textured crowns, whitish sapwood,
Dried up, resin pours from the Sal wood pores.

After ceremonies have stopped their ears,
The tree spirits wash and swing on tribal
Hopes, a branch of the Sal tree, then peace
Becomes more than a word; a simple lift off.

Then the breadth of wing, then the soar,
Then the landing of broad leaved forests, wet
On your Eastern side, with orchids, bamboo,
And creepers, almost wilting in your arms.

The wild Himalayan cherry in seasons full
Sharp and of cold hearts, rises a hundred feet;
Pale pink, its eyes heavy around its glossy ringed
Barks, decline to its ovoid yellow fruit turned red.

Ornamental as all fancy strikes. Then nature
Brings peace in the Silent Valley of Swachhand,
This is the truth of the poet, truth stumbling,
Within the reign of peace. It is yours alone.

Then those alder trees sigh as they lose
Their unstrung leaves, transfigured one by
One, convulsed, nitrogen fixing, stumble,
As their hearts tighten, serrated.

Then alternate with the cardomoms growing
Under their restful alder gaze; their synergetic
Energy consumed, locked by ancient kindnesses,
A flameless heat deep in your mountainous heart.

While aromatic, evergreen cinnamon trees
Turn violet pale, crumble silently into their dry,
Spicy sweet odors; leathery leaves that push through
Oils that dance; through their barks, a frenzied drum.

And what fragrance filled grasses meet your wielding
Shoulders! Bold and bolder, the chameleon plants,
Anxious in their perennial herb growth. Fish mints
That grow ever wary in their tyrant moods.

Hushed in their fragrance, the bay trees afloat
In their silvery gray barks, puncture the strident
Signals of Campbell's magnolia, bare branches end
At cream scented flowers, a lonesome sight.

The silk underside of smooth oval leaves,
Lick, or the heavy blooming saucer magnolias
Dull the brain, hybridize it even; sculpted
In your arms, cusped within the pedestal of time.

Now tall as the treed Cathcart's magnolia,
Now small as the Dwarf magnolia, or the evergreen
Temple magnolia, their young twigs and buds
Outspread in elliptical leaved stillness.

Then grow like those Egg magnolia, curved
Audacity of large velvet leaves, serene yellow flowers
Egg shaped before opening their buds, nor will
The grossness of nature complain, their bounty.

Saucer magnolia, white pink cuplike flowers,
hybrid of two Asian magnolias, uphill, their
Enlarged spirits rush together, leaping, laughing,
Spreading, until doomed to a deciduous fate.

Those hill peppers, hardy woody climbers,
Whisper love songs from Bhutan to Kumaon,
Nestled in love within their elliptical leaves,
Jarred response of some fantastic colors.

And there are the digital leaf divisions,
Within the Devil's tongue, an eight inch long
Spathe, rose in the throat voodoo lily,
Corpse flower, as the land folds down the valley.

If magnificence is a reality, it is the
Rhododendron forest aflame, twisted and gnarled,
The Spanish moss clings to its trunks, with so much
Guilt, as the forest opens to a broad hillside.

The elephant cobra lily bursts forth,
Its purple spathe sweeps through the
Air that restores, ringed in by the green world,
It protrudes, erecting above the hood, gasping.

In meadows and over mossy rocks, their coyness,
Of lily forms holds them together. The Cobra
Lilly dances with its white striped spathe; the hooded
Lance shaped leaflets of Yellow Cobra lily spurs.

The touch, wrinkled, bizarre, like the
World at large, spathes borne at ground
Of Griffith's Cobra Lily, its willing soul
Transpires, its mottled spathe, its leaf stalk

And on their leaning shoulders, grow more,.
Jaquemont's Cobra lily, the Curved hood and
The Whipcord Lily, the Sikkim Cobra Lily, a
Broken necklace of eternity, hammering.

Unusual shade loving Voodoo Lily, purple
Green foul smelling flower, meticulous in its
Hold of its vase like spike. Corpseflower, its
Heart parceled and parted, its speckled stem.

Its life blood, straight as a path of gold,
Even as the Indian grass Lily deflowers,
Unashamedly proud of its parentage, stem
Clasping, sheathing, perennial in its inadvertency.

You hold your orchids so well, they would
Triumph and hoot at the call of any prophecy!
Joseph's Herminium take a terrestrial measure,
Destined, in their basal, fleshy way, to your soul.

Those pink purple emotions rise, branched or simple,
On the slender Anthogonium; elations of the forest
Blooms. Fragrant, foxtail waxy, the Many Flowered
Fox brush Orchids is a balm or a beauty, commingling.

A clump forming small Warty Acampe orchid clings,
Warm, single stemmed, stoutly erect, notched
Leaves, orchids with large hearts and with small;
You give them the root and their tempered soul.

Your outer ridge loosens the girth, sap of the
Mind, of the eucalyptus swaying in the alpine
Breeze, nodding, dragging themselves upright,
Their barks peeling, floating across your bulges.

The bamboo grass, angel headed clumps,
Ornamental jazz sticks, stern and steady like
You, your mountainous witness, the dwindling,
Then the wild, strong, ready to root scaffoldings.

Like children gathered to frolic, the crimson
Rhododendrons sit on their perpetual thrones;
Now pale purple, now mingling with the lantana,
Wild flowering, splay tongued, thickly busy.

The Frangipani forces upon you its crooked trunk,
Its stubby branches a virtue; sweetly scented,
White flowers that spill their white milk juice;
Big leathery leaves taper, nipping between.

FIVE

NESTING

The bar necked geese fly above
Your ravines; there are no shadows,
The birds' cries, soundless, no season,
No shadow, only a vigorous flapping.

Hyperventilate, sternly wishing to hasten,
The bar necked geese fly higher above you;
Cherish their flighty existence, use short, rapid
Breath, then presage the birth of new oxygen.

Larger lungs lighten up their flight,
Melt into your mountainous heavens;
Flap, flap, their silver wings, expand
Blood capillaries, their spirits deceive.

Their mitochondriatic heat nestled in wings,
So deep and luxurious, so singly mutated,
Hyper define their haemoglobin, match it
Against your own long necked strength.

Still you would rise, and the golden eagles
Rise with you in their golden brown plumage.
Almost as if fate had approved them lording
As birds of prey, upturned, unlooping

The Himalayan golden eagles, tranquil
Within the blaze of their sharp talons; the
Very mirror of speed, soaring, unhurried,
Their powerful feet mixed with the eye.

Of agility. With long gliding motion, fly
Along your steep crags and precipices, by
The pale dull pallor of your desolation. High
Mountains ringing with powerful wing beats.

Amid spores stunted vegetation, they nest,
As if they would choose to climb the roof,
In high places, breeding under the mystical
Blue skies; these falcons in fiendish glee.

Predatory birds of honor bound dread;
Hurtling new born lambs down your sharp
Cliffs, nibbling their remains in studied delight,
Down dark brown and golden napes, fast gliding action.

Diving in with spectacular display,
They needs must tear apart pigeons,
Snowcock, chukor, pitifully over the
Swinging avian food of your pheasants.

Your Himalayan eyes look with desolate wonder,
As they gobble down crows. Their unhurried, rugged
Soaring speed, kill Tibetan argali lambs, home
Range young ibex, marmots and hares.

The fawns of musk deer and ghorals,
Wither under their mystic rapture, their
Silent flapping flight. Stretch their pale nape
Patch of glory, sense of territoriality, perhaps.

Endangered by all our need to counter,
Their aerial conflict, raptors in their timeless
Moments, booted eagles of falconry-delight,
A rush of pure adrenaline. No bird of freedom.

Do the warblers stand a chance against
Such might? Carry the mighty memories of you,
Your mountainous passes, pouring the colors
Of their warbled songs on their broad bills.

You are always turning, responding,
To the thrilling of the yellow vented warbler,
No other movements, nor would the rufous throated
Wren warblers dare your martial build.

So would the rusty throated wren babbler sing as,
It heads suddenly toward the riverbed, carved,
Sinuous limbs of a waterfall aching to the sounds of
Tawny breasted wren babbler, or snow throated ones.

Counter your stern look, the striped laughing thrush
Chestnut throated, brings out antiphonal sounds,
Alternate their songs with the clouds that fly, in
Soulful rhymes, across your lines, high, higher.

Nor compete with the slender black headed jay,
As the dews quiver over you, chilling. Blackness
Cresting the Himalayan bird's tremulous screech,
Long pauses between, on open grounds within you.

And the hoary throated barwings respond, "wiu uu,"
Quavering, foraging, preening, striking long crown
Feathers, as the morning light sifts through moist
Montane forests, cover your thick Himalayan hide.

Your restful mornings begin with soundless tweets,
The black winged tit, spot winged, black crested,
Choke the heart with delight; mingle, then diminish,
The yellow cheeked tit's flighty delights. In breeding.

Agile feeders, deaden the suffering, of insects and of
Spiders, run your fingers in woodpeckers' holes,
Driven to a tumult, ride high through the forest
Canopies, excavate their silence, through yours.

The Verditer Flycatcher sits on you,
Reflecting, at its appointed time, commenting
On your abundant glory, your empire of
Verdant muscles, unlocked, in its reflections.

As winter unfolds, the white capped water redstart,
Sings its diffident, often dissonant songs, sadly happy,
As your mountain streams disappear, now shining in
White light, as its breeding eggs break, undulating.

Looking toward its own partially fanned tail,
Whistle a melody to your upside down state,
Its drooping wings seeking self-destruction,
Along your ferociously large boulders.

The rather large white winged Red Starter,
Also refusing to be admonished, stare through
The bent branch, indifferent to its own white crown,
Picking up memories of your alpine meadows.

Its upper breast blackness, match the
Evening shadows. White patches on its wings,
Slamming, the engraved look on you, for
Centuries, then examine your rocks, for fruits.

While the enormity of insects consumed,
Glisten on the plumage of the blue tail, their
Blueness, snapped by the stiff winds, those that
Blow over your and the devouring, bush robins.

And your high mountain passes live separate
Lives from the tiny fowl; blood pheasants that
Sink their strong black bill into your streaming
Morning air, their corrosive gray backs flushed.

Short tailed, move in convoys over your
Coniferous scrub lands, as distance reveals the
Colors of their dark ash plumage, weighted over
By lance shaped feathers, uncompromisingly straight.

Red feet, the glorious stuff of red around the eyes,
As your mountain heads are swamped with light,
So does redness strike a match to their throats, their
Foreheads, against your snow white conflagration.

Where the snow pigeons fly swiftly, hopeful
To let more of their wise talk drop down your
Rocky hill sides, the multiplicity of their forms
Scatter their morning climbs with your touch.

Their black heads and snow white neck collars,
Intermingle with hill pigeons and rock pigeons
Beyond the snowdrift, your sequestered valleys,
Starkly recall forgotten old love songs.

Roost in the sad nooks and grammar of your
Cliffs, while they seemingly sleep still; their
Shyness runs in loops, amid your large gaps, so
They can breed in colonies, marooned crevices.

Their unkempt nests laid within the realm of thought,
Inside the ledges of rocks, interlaced, as you disappear,
With sticks and grassy shoots, as you pose regretting,
The bewildered affection thumping within.

So would the laughing thrush move, amid
Your glacier like shape shiftings, carved in your
Own melt, in brief promises, its black cap and
Band in brief promises, on its brown tail.

While the heavy parts of you match, in spiked
Shapes, the heaviness of the griffon vulture, sameness
Defines your brown undersides. The vulture's
Greed, pale streaked, perched on your crags.

Your lower regions smothered, by the crested
Serpent eagle, brown and spotted between the
Furrows of its obliging lips, kissing you, or
Rather, obliging snakes and serpents. Sated.

Its spotted belly seems to sing, in rhythmic
Steps, a distinctly unruly scream, treble notes,
Of cheel grandeur, sitting upright, feed, feed away.
Until time to perform breeding acrobatics once more.

The Great Cormorant, its brown forehead hitting
Its own agenda, of nests on the warm ledges of your
Lakes that touch, like white wine, a ribbon drifting
Into the rapid moves of your streams, obliging.

Fish that it sucks out, crow like, on your banks,
Glistening blue black plumage, fanning it dry,
To the ground, wings wide open, a drifting current
Its almost exclusive casualty, of yellowness.

Hovering above your peaks, the black winged kite,
With quiet discernment, descends, kestrel like,
Make a luscious meal of the field mice and lizards
That seem do much a part of your flexible green.

And the crested honey buzzard, whistles loud,
As its glad times arrive, perched on your treetops.
Single pitched, insatiable habit of flying, encircling,
Honey bees, or even wasps and their tender larvae.

The small dark quail, an unnoticed loss,
In the confusion of what has vanished from
Your valleys, even as the blown rain brings,
Memories of your extinct winged divisions.

The strange dark eyes of the bay owl, speak,
And again speak, unusual looks, short rounded,
Nocturnal, melancholic flued whistles. Only
The fields know, in perpetual shades of darkness.

The jackdaw loves the details configured
In bright and shiny metaphors. Scattering
Its wings, it comes to understand its impossible
Nature in your serene and raw activations.

In the closing and opening of the eyes,
There is so much between, hapless additions,
Notwithstanding, birds aloft, flying high,
And animals passing by, inhabiting you.

The Himalayan Monal pheasant fancies its
Chances are good, with digging practices that
Attach insects and roots to tubers; vibrant green crest,
Coppery feathers, white rump that gasps in beauty.

An alpine euphoria sets in, as the black necked
Tibetan crane twists and turns, consume barley and
Wheat, as your trees rustle and whisper, in a sort
Of weak chorus, as your green valleys echo.

As the sky clears above you, to a watery blue,
The hairy wild yak summons its largesse; large
Body giving its meat and milk to hungry humans,
Unspoken, unbeaten, drooping head, mute.

The wild yak's wildness is a ruse; here in your
Mountains, it is domesticated enough, as if across
A panel of sunlight. The warm ride on its back,
Cuts down on its incessant, solitary dyings.

Graze quietly on your herbs and lichen,
Crushed now in the bowels of your snows,
In spite of its dense undercoat, soft, close-matted;
Hunted down, in the cold heavy air of greed.

Your highlands and plateaus would weep,
For the long shaggy hair of the wild yak, finely
Filtered by death's irrational demands. An alpine
Beauty shattered, poached by the careless smile.

Hybridized, domestic and wild yaks intermingled,
Like a folded towel, shamefaced, diseased, without
Navigation, absolved of its own habitat, to clamber,
Nimble-footed over rough terrain, in single file.

Every animal has its story in your mountainous
Dwellings, like marmots, little mammals engulfing
Your flowering plants, new roots and leaves teething,
The squirrel like marmot sees echoes of its future.

Your rugged, wooded hills and slopes stay
Undisturbed by the wild goat, like an unvoiced
Series of syllables, goat shaped, long brown hair,
Straggle down as purposeful intrusions, on you.

When the cow-goat like Takin tramps the leaves,
They lie tangled, like sad dreams, beneath the strong
Horn of the Takin, stocky creature of your high valleys,
As it runs them down, bulky, cattle-chamois-like.

Caught underfoot, its lustrous golden coat looks
Up to the ripped-up golden sky, stretch on hind legs,
Eating together in groups of twenty, through bamboo
Thickets, secrete the strong oily smells, Takin like.

The Himalayan Tahr, like outgrown shoes, even Toed,
Rubbered core, small headed mammal, thick reddish
Wool coats, the ghosts of its thinning coat gone,
Shedding its hair, without navigation, without internalization.

The blue sheep, so alluring to the dreams,
Of its predators, camouflage, blend into
Your rocky parts, scamper up and down,
Feed and rest on your grassy mountain slopes.

Your trees rustle, then whisper, quiet
Witnesses to the bluish sheen of the blue
Sheep, better known as bharal, at the rutting,
Opening and closing. Tending, blocking.

Shimmer and hiss, until nature takes its
Natural course; between horns short and
Curved, like moustache loose on its hinges,
Then downed by the snow leopard, vengefully.

The marbled cat walks across your slopes,
As if and almost loving you the wrong way,
Stocky, short-legged creatures of glory, touching
Your cold mountainous air, impaled, adapted.

Along with the phosphorescence of pale grey eyes,
The snow leopard waits, for the echo in your green ears.
Its thick fur, tanned yellow, discolorations of smoky gray
Hide, dappled with black open rosettes.

Wide paws, fur on the underside to grip your steep
Hilly terrain, those discrete moments as the snow
Leopard sees the intermittent light, breathe your thin
Air, its roar snagged, ossified by laryntial absentia.

And so it quietly hisses and chuffs, its long thick
Tail balanced, vigilance defined, mewing, growling
And wailing, in intense poetic capitulations, cover its
Face with its furry tail, sleep in the syllables of rocks.

Climbing up your meadows and rocks, shift your
Cold intimations, in crepuscular measuring distances,
As solitary as your twilight hours, or camouflaged
Within the transparent light of dawn's light wings.

And so, inevitably sleep haunted, nor implicit,
In its scent marks, secretive operations of urine
Dust, closures defined, territorial within sheltered
Patches of your rocks, riddled bullets of livelihood.

A sense of failing, or is it opportunism that prolongs
The big cat's desire for its non-definitive acts,
Carnivorously putting down, feeding on carrion,
Livestock, bharal, argali, and horses, deer and panda.

Except for the shaggy high altitude cow, the yak.
Shy and reserved messengers of the gods, for whom
All mythology becomes a time-lapse. On sturdy legs,
Rounded cloven hooves, leftover streak, wild, erratic.

Across your snow-filled passes, over hushed tracks
Of long yak caravans, between the delicacy of balancing
Loads of cargo, and the warnings against slipping,
Its well trained bulky frame, like a river rising.

The bells and bright red tassels on the lead yak,
Respect for authority, the treacherous paths and trails,
Their owner's commands, cross without faltering steps
High altitude, quiet eyes flecked, and the bells tinkle.

Giving, always giving, like gods, about fulfilment,
Milk from female yak, spinning in the air, from the
Long fiber wool to its own meat, giving, in months
On your abrasive snow and ice, its warmth anew.

Farming, herding, making yak dung briquettes,
Or selling fur of the red panda, an unnoticed lapse.
The acrobatics of a dissolving noon, as needs change,
The bamboo eating red panda is compromised.

Its bear shaped body, an integument of thick
Russet fur, skillful and shady recesses of trees,
The Nepalese 'ponya' chews away at plants,
Its long bushy tail balancing its phrases.

Carry a panda head on the body of a cat,
Its future invasive, under the thick disguise of
Your deciduous and coniferous forests, hanging
on bamboo poles, red fox red in the cold morning sun.

Nor endure the cute eyes of the teddy bear
Looking giant panda. It hides in your dense
Bamboo trees, its hunger a surfeit of its fury,
Its white and black fur, a strange piecework.

Then the cameras would steal time, to shoot
At the shy musk deer, munch quietly on your
Leaves and grasses. The surprise of its slow ending
Is no surprise, trapped by its own scent gland.

Endangered by its own curse, its given possibilities
Latent only in the male musk deer. Stay far from
Human habitation, without antlers, broad toed
Stocky adaptation, Of your high altitudes.

Poached surprise of aromatic endings,
The unknowables and mysteries of hunters using
Snares, the undoing of female deer and its young,
Sedentary life ends; static cries in abdominal musks.

The rhetoric of silence also turns over, the Himalayan
Black and brown bear, jump down, falling over as a
Violent catapult, omnivorous as a stolen sentence.
Gaze on as your animals disappear, mute witness.

SIX

DENUDING

Root rot is a real offense, wasted;
Human life supports it, as much as
Pathogens, induced, inducted, acridly,
Into the grand scheme of exposed all, snapped.

Conditions that attack and corrode, coffin length,
Just as the human soul becomes compressed,
Shrewd as fungal pathogen, gouged, piteous,
Eat, eat, no pause, then eat.

When conifers become susceptible,
They kneel, then part, broken, limb waiting,
By bitter limb. The caustic, stressed effects
Shake these mountains, limbering, grieving.

Bend, move, break, austere trunks
Crack, old and mature trees moldy, enclosed,
Disagree with each other, then hunched,
Send apocalyptic screams through the bellies.

Of mountains that are not made
Of glass, though the winds of chaos
Attack. The growth of roots stopped,
As winds change direction, cascading.

The fungus keeps chewing, until their
Lascivious eyes ache. The sun climbs
Higher above the mountains, hot,
Then hotter, almost like a leaking juice.

The Himalayan cypress cries in pain,
Its hollow cavities shrink from excess water,
At the bottom of mountain slopes, its itch
Becomes feverish, warm, then warmer.

The winds pull the trees, a different
Kind of frequency directs their crowns.
While their trunks get carried into
The eye of the wind, then founder, fall.

Anatomy is an internal matter,
For life becomes unstructured
Climate change unsettles, the trees,
Resonate, pulled in diverse fashions.

Trees and mountain plants suffer,
Life spans change as climates change,
Pests and pathogens eat up an inner core,
Slender stems, elastic, fell, fallen.

When optimum conditions fail,
When bark beetles and fungus prey,
When winters become warm, then
Mildness becomes a cause, more tragic.

In Bhimtal, in other mountain towns,
A crash and a crack echo cracks within
Mountain survival, the mountains rise,
They erupt, like Gods in lava fashion.

Deep ruts in heavily eroded trails, life
Is the soil that has stopped groping, molested,
It opens its parched lids, looks around, at
The thatched huts perches on ridge crests, appalled.

No one has shattered your gentle flow of time
As land slides that come to your green mountains,
Gentle concoctions as much as umbilical ghosts,
Of your body and mind collapsing as antipodes.

To harness electric power from your rivers,
It is like carrying your hands around your hair,
Water pooling, crochet-necked fury, rubble expands,
Brilliant lung power, submerged hydropower stations.

Blast luciferous holes, destroy highways, lakes
Meandering, blasting forth, like an incestuous
Framed matter, gauging, swelling, exploding,
Wounded beyond contention into floods, unheaded.

Landslides bury people, into a lonesome dark,
Thralled by mud and debris, what must develop
In urban fashion, setting your world on its own
Haunches, puncturing force of nature's sad fury.

Damaged roads and highways offer a fraught
Story of neglect, bones on bones of ripped mountain
Passes, empty display cases of coherence, as if death
And damaged infrastructure are one and all.

Those terrible yarns spun out of colluding,
Colliding waters, damaged bewailing spaces,
Flushed out miracles squeezed between riverine soft
Sloped breasts, and your spiked pinnacles, flushed.

Your young geology plays games, certain words and
Phrases that move your earth, emerge with seismic
Intent; hillslopes angled in a tight embrace, tend
To cloudburst, collapsed agricultural terraces muse.

Weakened by land slide upon land slide, a noose
Exists with your geodynamics, collapsed road cuts,
Fall like errant teeth, channel incisions become a set
Of revisions, unsloped, flapping recognitions.

Human impact acts ferociously on your inherent
Weaknesses; the waters suck at your faults.
Appendages glare angrily; channel incisions are
Coitus interruptus, Unfamiliar as empty night dreams.

The sediment load of your rivers' destiny
Proclaim, like drenched oracles, the carnivore
Nature of an appetite whetted by boulders,
Still tending, still erosion mechanisms.

Nothing rhapsodizes so sternly as flash floods,
The sudden surge of water has a music all its own,
Sing quietly along a riverbed, an intervening portent,
Or a dry gully; rise, rise, in force and sadistic volume.

Neither predict nor avoid, carry the burden of rocks,
Sing with the debris of invasive sounds, as blue skies
Watch, solemnly. Flash floods break silence of your
Mountain catchments; a purposeful, vivid intensity.

Neither time to prepare nor avoid their evocations,
Flash floods foretell an ardor, lasting minutes, or
Days, intricately and divinely disordered death,
Change watersheds, like a destructive stalker.

Your steep slopes bewail their spaces, to
Flush themselves out. Surface erosion becomes
A dangerous catcher, angling this way or that,
Changing climate, and the configuration of it.

Becomes a hillflesh clouding, summer rains
Prowl metaphor heavy, exhume precipitation,
Spitting heavy, condensed. Vulnerable as the
Hills gone fatter, then explode, with emptiness.

Huge boulders move with fury, destroy trees
Astounding you, your canyons, tear out bridges
Across feasts that ring with homicidal fury, as your
Earth hardens, coughing out fields, inverted.

Thunder and hail are locked like bumpers,
Anguish builds dreams, panic-stricken, a tide
Of aftertaste blends its shape, as the waters recede,
Your unstable terrain shakes, shudder, river valleys.

Rock, mud, sediment, hillside collapse, inundate,
Downed transmission lines, hazard your landscape,
Your snow filled mountains body forth rivers,
Rivers, silted, polluted, as tired forests yawn.

Ponder, helpless, neither bath nor drink your
Choked waters, look into the eyes of dredge,
Like ghosts without their sheets, untreated,
Raw sewage offers optical illusions, disaffected.

If dredging was a simple act of turning,
An endless succession of moments deposited,
Dumped from the unwanted dark, culled haphazard,
Navigation channels framed, tempted from harbors.

Waters drawn out endlessly, a desperate urge
To urbanize, roll back that film, exploit vanity,
Until it descends to its last breath, fueled by pelf,
That sweat of the human soul remade, rebooted.

Spinning off climate change, jostling with forests,
Denuded by the annual rites of hype and fervid awe,
Shrunk through time and space, bolstered by glacial
Acts of disappearance, speared by time.

When water bodies become land masses, when
Forest floors trail, undesired, bleeding conversations
Recur, between suspended sediments and more,
Particles that seem ashamed, then seek redress.

Begrimed with twilight blues, the wetlands
Vanish with foul-mouthed fury, their memory
Becomes a lens; under low precipitation content,
The land hardly knows when it becomes a morgue.

Preserve, preserve, through knots of thorough pain,
Voiced down to the shadowy remnants their high
Ecological value, like wings trapped against open
Water surfaces, sustained, relentlessly, reclaimed.

If deforested is what you waited for, stripped, burned,
Then lean over into your living, vital estuary again;
If the clever ascent of increased wastelands and
Alien weeds strike, then would you feel the doom.

If you have not pictured your own death, languish,
Then would you slice the clouds to bring back with
Gusto, lost species, rare wild life, the musk deer, monal
Pheasant, gibbons and tigers, rhinos, pushed out.

As if extinction were a one trick pony, only a subtle
mechanism tumbling down to rest, then rise again,
In a forbidden night of consummation, the snow leopard
Would redraw itself, dance with the river dolphins.

Burned clean, demand more fuelwood, as if timber
Were a fairy, weaving gold, in uncontrolled realms
Of intensified removals; the aftertaste of habitat loss
Is like smashed glass, glittering falsely away.

Hold the mask to subsistence farming, redraw the
Contours of sustainable air, careful not to break seal,
Half open your crutches, swing them back and forth,
Intensified erosion stands en pointe, in a state of shock.

In a chain of misassumed mechanisms, the trees
Look black, shiver in the cold air, feel molecular,
The canopy layers withhold, in mid-sentence, their
Sense of shattered neglect, accept frugal non-being.

The crown of trees feel, gently, like pulling of hair,
Intone a sense of restlessness, a peculiar sense of splash
Erosion, shattered and eroded, a kind of chorus set up to
The huge raindrops that weep through their sad tale.

Channel habitat loss in a noble clinging mode,
Frozen for months, kisses that were never received,
Confirm the need for forest clearance, affixed high,
In watersheds that drink, acres of widespread denial.

Replace by terraced fields of undulating grain,
It becomes an overly valorous dream, the insidious seed
Replaced, managed, creak nor shudder, trees stunted,
Lopped and split, as hollow, preconceived ideas.

Forest fires spread like molten melt,
Destroy your archetypal peace, poachers
In search of game, rouse and put to flight,
Putting all to sleep, leaf by leaf, molten.

Balls of fire spread, recklessly tripped,
Released, plopped over, gather firewood,
And ignite gravity's cuddled up dreams,
Nor cure resultant hunger, licking flames.

Seeing the flora and the fauna flicker, fall,
Spread along the ground, senescent leaves and
Twigs, dry grasses that engulf the world around,
Their insolent tails mock at human need.

Lightning strikes, bent over and duplicated,
The crowns of conifers the color of burning sun,
Burning logs downhill, spread its far crying noise,
Combust, naked flame upon dense vegetation cover.

Unheeded, a match struck, green light of underbrush
Spread, stealthily, quickened by breeze, fanned out,
Blazing woods, blackened forms of ecology, words
That care not; embers, of biodiversity, transparent.

SEVEN

MEDITATING

Rain in your rugged, soaring mountains
Defines peace; a creeping steady pause
In life's monumental wretchedness,
Tricky, trickle, then grudged peace again.

No thunder nor storm cries human meriting,
A swish, as life departs, gives broad room,
Breath by losing breath, chained to losing breath,
As the giant shadows of your overtures, loom.

Gray echoing monsters, larger than
Life, tender somewhat, a sugary stern
air about them, then the downpour,
Rocking the passion of the trapeze artist.

The mountains never sleep, or at least, they
Pretend not to. In the foothills, the sureness
Gone amuck, heedless of all, your primordial
Landscape that would rather loose a sound.

Unknown, sweeping joys, untouched by
Civilization's dirty hand, plunging so
They live in the folds, the valleys an
Expanse of kindness, glittering oracle, deft.

Those rotting, cracked stone images,
Carved in the lonely mindscape of
Paintings on the cypress crowned walls
A Hindu shrine, red, then sapphire.

Metal images twanging, stoical in Lahul
And Spiti, gleaming tailored, monasteries of
Utter romance, an itch that starved souls sense
with the coming wind, withered, Padmasambhava.

A quickening impulse, samadhi and
A short cocktail of ritual, hieratic costumes,
Cuts their design by half, loosen on an empty sky,
Their bubbling selfhood, and out of it.

Larger than those looming giants,
The temple bell sounds, faint wings,
Of doubt drifting, the rebel devoutly strikes,
An open window shuts down on Du-khang.

Uncannily placed high above in Spiti Valley,
Kye Gompa soars among the golden gateway
Of the stars, withstand the chasmed attack of
Enemies, human and natural; intertwine charity.

Soaring and dipping, a training ground for monks,
Locking stone for stone, paintings and murals, shielded
By Buddha images, the shadows of others long past,
Kadampa, Tabo, Drangtse, Hikim, meditators watching.

Your rivers fold back, the blue Bhaga and the Chandra,
Studded among the unpretentious structures, single
Storied, bland externality, nor ornament nor guile,
Scriptural renderings that feel the enclasping flow.

Great Lotsaba offered healing against your stern
Renderings, stupendous in the bliss of the Dharma;
If clarity lies in the mandala design of our lives,
Perfect, unwilling, spiritual prototypes of your kind.

The dwarfed pagodas of Guru Ghantal monastery,
Test the reality of ancient trade routes, stiffen their
Sinews, with embellished murals, fine painted ceilings,
The magnificence, the concentric circles in mandalas.

Beyond the burden of the flesh, evacuating minds,
Darkness lifts your hills and valleys, Phugtal Gompa
Rises, chiseled in rich singularity, the imponderable
Cliff shaped the hungry breath of gorge, impenetrable.

As sharp winds buffet it, devoted lamas survive,
With neither grief nor without reason, for satiety,
Within a mud and stone structure, surviving like you,
The guiding spark of centuries, like you, unsleeping.

Neither in fantasy nor in feeble dreams, uncannily,
Meditating mountains join, transformed into restful
Thought, sprouting alpine limbs, beneath the shadow
Of monasteries and temples, housing gods, in enormity.

Striding proudly your vast shadows, hold communion,
Tsangpo monastery smiles archaically, neither look
Askance at Paro valley, nor second Buddha, mounting
Off a tigress, homily that brings answers within, retreat.

Where shadow of the Gods rest, those wise masters
Build esteem and give fashion of order, spiritual pursuit,
On summit of hills, gleaming in finery of Buddha.
The fluttering flags beckon to you, your pain divine.

Does Vajra motif symbolize your masked munificence?
Mystical dance dramas enacted by lamas, formless void
Spelled in stucco figures in Kardang and Shashur, learned
Looks, murals inspired by Jataka themes, ritual fantasy.

Sunyata radiates from the Buddha images, riddled
With your peace; ancient mandala stares many handed
Demoniac images. Reflect angry moods of harsh winter
The lamaistic lore rings your rugged mountains.

Spin wheels of destiny, conical structures, pulled
Into empty spaces outside monasteries, thwart misfortune
Rolls of thin paper, entwine mantras on Mani wheels, Tibetan Chants
Wound around axle, Om Mani Padme Hum, papered over.

Nor with no less rigor, Vedic Hinduism resounds
A long walk from a Hindu temple in the frosty air;
Centuries have invaded the cracks; filled with plaster,
Stop the fervent longings; genius leaks in slow brush.

Coughed out in creations, Kedarnath temple rises
Through the aureate sky; an old abode of Shiva; and
Mandakini river, snaps out, cascading force, bemused,
Through the foothills of your windy, aspiring cliffs.

The Pandavas held a portion of their weight, their
Sins absolved, caught in a triangular wind, Kedarnath
Remote under the crescent sun, snow clad
Mountains and glaciers amazed, divine miracles.

On a plateau whose gentle droop and sway, brilliant
And burdened, a Nandi observes, imagined out of a
Rock, carved from out of a dream; graceful like the
Pandav-dance, the tribals dance to the cold, cold beat.

A thumb falling from off the face of heaven, the
Mysteries of light, become a Shiva linga, and rub
Ghee on your linga, paid for in remorse and sorrow;
If only water could wash off human guilt, prolonged.

Where birds behave like your mountains, at the same
Kedarnath temple, Shiva remains forever, the horizons jagged
Amid your snow peaks, and Mahesha burns like a lamp,
Fill spaces of eternal light, Jyoti turned into Kedareshwara.

The gap between winter and fall becomes an
Enlightened span; the deities at the temple displayed,
Like your extractable elements, when worship becomes
A mode of sustenance, a perfect stamp for the soul.

So does Madikini river flow, an utter and placid pace,
Snake through the foothills of your mountains that
Sees tiny blossoms. The realm of rising fury that flashed
Through Kedarnath temple and river rising, only stunned.

A black stone statue of Badrinarayan in your Garhwal hills,
A protected Vishnu inside Badrinath temple; gazing at his
Gilded gear are two sons, Nar and Narayan, your namesakes;
So does Alaknanda river snake around, snug in your bosom.

A conch, a wheel, gold canopy of a Badri tree, black statues,
Kubera, Narada, Adi Shankara, a temple of such mold stands
Apart, hot sulphur springs tumble, within your strength,
Dissolved and moved, stroke your ego, by a long haul.

Nestled in your chest, ten thousand feet high, Adi
Shankara set the brushwork for Badrinath temple;
The precision of a dream, an incredible child built it,
And so the Nambudiris paid for their priesthood.

Where the Indian jujube grows, with a unique sense
Of its own subjectivity, surprised by your stern visage,
Goddess Lakshmi sates her lord's hunger with the Badri,
Amid the crackling heaviness of the Himalayan cold.

And senses come alive, a dip in the Yumnotri; attain
Moksha, dense forests erupt from me, waterfalls that
Sacred ponds, Yumnotri temple, the Chardham quest,
Echo the sounds of nature around you, your pilgrim soul.

A princess built the temple; Yama blossoming forth
Yumnotri high above in your protective shade. Trek the
Green clavicle of Hanuman Chatti. Dense green forests
Overpower the gnawing ache of the feet, and the soul.

Like a broken lava flow, devotion brings surging
Crowds; the holy baths hook the heart, hum tunes
To the sacred quality of Suryakund. The sheen of
Warm water, flopped, faltered, fatigue a paintbrush.

The early evening air cools Gaurikund and Suryakund
Carved up to a warmth where devotion blends in,
Dip the small sack of rice; incomprehensible exchange
Of prayer and prasadam; an exquisite aspect of the soul.

The rare Brahma lotus blooms somewhere, veiled,
The lip of its light cascading on your broad breasts,
Somewhere along the path to the Hindu shrine, in your
Guts, the weary pilgrim soul hopes, for a tiny miracle.

Sacredness flows from within you, the Yumnotri
Glacier squirms under the weight of such intense faith;
Near your Bandarpunch peaks, tumbling in clear water,
Flocking forth, renewed, for a new world order.

Is it small? Is it really so? Undulant wavelengths of
Spiritual longings emerge; Chhota Char Dham pilgrimage
As the tiny magnet throbs within, with gagged hearts,
Hindu souls trace the purpose of life on your head.

The Saptarishi kund stares, unafraid, against the
Backdrop of sickle shaped moraines, like a book
Opened, its crystal blue waters stare back, its pebbled
Banks aching for that dreaming display of the lotus.

High up in your big chained embrace, Gangotri temple,
Whitewashed, the whip and virginal flame of a Goddess,
Ganga rises, a figured brocade from Gangotri glacier;
Cleansing in magnificence, so much sacrality abounds.

An unforetold storm burst, a Ganga touched earth, the
Stream of life released from its brilliant lungs, Bhagirath's
Penance stalks her puncturing fall, and Shiva flushes
It wisely in his locks, like a coiled interruptus.

Tending the austere penance, set upon its odd
Haunches, Ganga returns, an illumination of gold,
Its sparkling bones rejuvenated at Gangotri temple,
Freeing souls, fraught with love in a red palanquin.

You would bewail the deodar and pines, bones upon bones,
bright knifings into your soul, an incestuous wound bleeds,
As Ganga rushes through your gorges, tossing around, rocks
Of such astounding matter, and the temple stands, inviolate.

Placate her wrath with a claim on eternity, unravel its mystery,
The priests carry water to Shiva, benediction soothing his throat;
The Garhwal hills wonder, shaking out sunlight after the rains,
White granite Gangotri stands erect, surround Shivaling, its footprints.

Your head bowed, a glimpse inside a cave shrine,
Lost amid your spear points, desire awakens, inside
Amarnath temple; Shiva explains the mysticism of life,
Immortal dreams cohere within an ice Shiva lingam.

A face reflected in the mirror, dim the illusion of life,
Celestial nectar to Parvati, wincing at pleasure, roofed
Stalagmite whose fountains are within, synchronize with
The moon waxing and waning; ice formations of the mind.

Amid your dreaming imagination, there are others, as
Kalpeshwar, where your bone chilling cold does not deter
The matted tresses of Shiva; the hump of your heads stretched
Far by Panch Kedar. Your back humped into caves, time lapse

Of mystical Shiva Lingam, linked fragments. Shiva, angry
Track of crackle, found in Rudranath temple, his devotees
Feel the tender arch of emotion, extractable elements; disguised
Bull, blended and masked, Shiva's idol gets a royal bath.

Unpaired above us, your artists' brushwork breathe life
Into Shiva's face. Chandrashila peak gazes at the evening altars,
Lips glued and meditative, lacquered coats of eight metals,
Ashtadhatu that refuses to surrender to a new metaphor.

And Rudraganga flows quietly by, as mourners perform
Rituals for their dead, pind offerings to sate. Beyond the silence,
Your peaks perched high above, fuzzy fleshed, Nanda Devi,
Nanda Ghunti, Devasthan, Hathi Parbat, Trisul, all look upon

With sacramental silence at Rudranath; a river and a cave,
All bow to Shiva lore, in the hoary mountain swords light.
Shiva's arms evoke splendor amid your highest bones,
Faith that is not ruffled by your cold, unbreathable.

At Tungnath temple a black rock lingam rests, whirring
Weights of Pandava, time that gnaws at his self incarnated.
Paternal grace; hands that bespeak holy rage. A painful breach.

Yet another Shiva abode in Garhwal Himalayas,
Madhyamaheshwar Temple, sits in humble awe,
A navel shaped lingam within, dilation darkened;
And the green meadows outside ponder, surprised.

By their wobbly might, those sky kissing mountains,
Seamless, burdensome. Somewhat as in a timecard,
Neelkanth temple spreads piety through dense forests,
Nettled in a loop, blended Har Narayan mountain range.

Crescent shiverings of light, Pauri Garhwal lets loose
A web you cannot sift through. Lord Shiva consumes
Blue poison inside. An architectural ambiguity. Faith startled
The devotees seek union with your rugged, steep slopes.

Summer unfurls rhododendrons, as Sikh and Hindu
Pilgrims grasp the orb of light on Hemkund lake,
Break apart the rippling sound of waterfalls, glowing
Like Hemkund Sahib Gurudwara, crystal quaint.

Faith of all hue congregates, brightly festooned, scattered
In your hills and vales. You have slick escarpment, unblended,
Opened to love of the divine. The immaterial is glimpsed in
White domed Hazratbal Masjid near Dal lake, resilient beauty.

As in Amarnath shrine, trailing into your span. And yet,
Shiva's dazzling laughter blends your stretched,
Triangular leaps, Pashupati and you, Himalayas, fuse,
A protecting deity, ascetic of worldly dust, shriven.

Diving and flying Nataraja. Shiva's laughter echoes
In your hills and dales, rhythmically creating and
Destroying a cosmos, not blinded by your vast horizons.
Lambent, silver twisting ropes, radiating your options.

EIGHT

SYMBOLIZING

Your tall peaks see, how your people become
A part of you, your fingers and theirs, a seamless,
Soul smooth growth, of human gestures, your bones
And theirs, a narrative of mingling cultures, broad shade.

A part of you, a part of your silver deodar needs, simple
Prayers carved on monastery stones, your shadow fanned
Across curled lips of bells, as women carry their heavy loads,
Their faces disappear into your being, your masked conical head.

Simple mountain cultures, dangling out of simple singing
Syllables, happy as the wind blowing through your spaces,
Insisting on a simple way of life, like the glittering lights,
On your tumultuous back, twilight penetrating, clinking.

Your killer peaks gyrate under the burden of those
Voices, layers of modernity hide the truth, their porous
Selves smothered, like the heavy load of hides carried on
Their backs, their truths reshaped into spanking new boots.

Against your shocking authenticity, against your shimmering
Silence, the desire to be disappears, for you will displace their
Dust into your bones, so they will relearn the art of simplicity,
You so well exude, amid your brightly feathered white glory.

Up the valleys they bound, into scattered legions of escape,
Through villages so accustomed to your warnings of sunrise,
High mountains that proudly wait, in fragile dignity, loose
Boulders and rocky trails that embellish, turning you over.

Walk the old trade routes, the Sherpas are carriers
Of pain, like yaks, bound to the purpose of life they never
Question; a necessary patch of your quiet dreamings, treasures
That load, piercing, nor ever experimenting with their karma.

From Solukhumbu, into your eastern fibrous highlands,
Sherpas shape fragments of their destiny, nomadic principles
That sniff storms, thrash your eye of danger; mountaineering
Skills measure hardiness, expertly swallow up your high altitudes.

Adapt themselves on the chipped edges of your passes, your peaks,
Jagged shapes rest in diluted lights, Sherpas are the well-shod
Genetic adjustors of your history, their haemoglobin binding pitch
Shuffled out to your moon charmed self, striving to blow kisses.

And so the Sherpas endure their search still for your pure-land,
Beyul, sacred as your valleys, Buddhist beliefs that last amid the
Deeper mysteries on the hard icicles of your rocks. Loose network
Of Tibetan Buddhism buried deep, the living and the dead.

From the immaterial to the material, from home spun wool and
Silk to lightening flash bareness; Sherpas wearing long sleeved
Robes, Chhuba, raatuk, kanam, kara, embossed, while you expand,
Grow tall, with natural feel of the snow, winds, clouds and rain.

In your embalmed mountain darkness, Sherpas search,
Deities and demons hiding in the quiet ecstasy of your
Forests, wild and stroking the heavens; appease them, convulsed
With reverence, lofty mothers of the world, sacred-sweet, protecting.

Lamas presiding over rituals, in the soft effulgence of sunlight
That peeps, ceremony after ceremony, tossed in the passive, mute
Indulgence of mercy, to mountain folks bewitched, an aching clench
Of the soul, supernatural chasms amid your spirit world passages.

Gompas that sit tight on your high ledges, away from the edge
Of doom, touched by iridescent communities of lamas, strong
Like you; faith that burns undying, annual festivals and readings
Of sacred texts, imbedded in the tall scepter of your thunder-stone.

Monks seek support beyond your looming mass, celibacy vows
Strung to the strong resolve, you dare take them on the path
Of knowing, the internal shift to search out truths you symbolize,
The endless bounds of billowing desire silenced by your might.

As birds fluttering high up in your being, so do faces flutter,
Ethnic tribes share their identity with your remote valleys,
Defoliated, cratered, changed beings, the Kinnars, Kilinds, and
Kiratas, mutated, cold fizz on the flesh of ethnic groups, shredded.

Faith split up, for those who dwell in your ghostly laughter,
Hindus, Buddhists, muslims, all winged flesh of the same salt,
And the same blood flowing, in the ionized cells of Nepalis, Bhutiyas,
And Lepchas, sharing each other's dreams, the mantle of your gaze.

In your triangulated arms, do the divisions of Negroid, Mongoloid,
Aryan tell us new falsehoods? You have no use for the scraps and
Bits of human divisions; your benedictions whisper new metaphors,
Surrender, like the last flare of the sunset, start from absolute scratch.

Creating and singing folks songs, did you break up the musk
Route? Did you grieve in the bright sunlight, when Kashmir
Gleamed; saffron and Bon Buddhist medicines melded, Balti folksongs
Produce quivers, tearful eyes, when Buddhists and muslims unwind.

You would sit there, quietly watch, Boddhisattva image-like,
Your dreaming eyes listen for something, deep inside the
Essence of Ladakhi songs, the winds ripping and moaning, with
So much love longing, through your rocky sternum, revived.

And so Pahadi folks possess you, squint at shades of moonlight;
Silver lines of dashes, you love, translate Himalayan festivals,
Raw rimmed, Mani Rimdu in your veins, unlaced by masked dancers,
Past strong definitions of starry impress, your forehead grown.

In your hands, the lights are turned on by sand drawings,
Your memory drifting down your rivers, inside their Mandala,
circle of life, bright colorful costumes, your spongy silences,
New modes of life, new technologies, new demons explode.

For some reason only you would know, the porters still lift,
Perpetuate the skeletal arms of our common humanity, across
Your green blanket, communicate fond love and friendship,
A flight of color invades, your long held secrets of their sacrifices.

So would you belong to your people, exhausted by sheer hardship,
So would you belong to them, exposed and inaudible; disciplined by
Proximate danger, your unnamed peaks painted by an aggrieved
Belief, an aversion to any replicas of your immense beauty.

So will they listen to your silent music, stirring agricultural
Wounds on your earth, profit from animal husbandry; history
Blows off your powerful repose; traders filter their commerce,
in frontier villages. Then weigh the circle of life, a strained flicker.

The wild storms buffet across your rock-charmed surfaces;
The Yeti circles and blots out the sun; Glacier Being, wild man,
Man or animal, the crypto being dares your radiant body puzzled,
A whistling swoosh sound, apelike, full blooded, buoyantly vacant.

Wandering in your wilderness, a cranking art, watching, reclusive,
Ribboning out large footprints in Barun valley, engulf the senses;
Mystical ceremonies appease your condensed awareness, so lush,
Fabulous, Yeti mythology confounds you, doubling crypto spirals.

Your long shadows back to back, tell us unspeakable truths,
If consciousness means, you are the watchful ghost, raising us
Toward you, with flooded lungs, an assemblage of our earth
Traditions, earth-feminine, fecund with its implacable history.

Fully aware, your message gulped beyond your ever expanding
Multiplicity; to meet your needs, we must give up ours,
To meet new heavens, move toward your excruciating silence,
Tipped further up, as if spiritual aspiration grows on your trees.

Between earth and heaven, what lies within the coils of your soul?
Why would your being bind our minds like chains, when those who
Dig themselves out, surrender, flee to your dissolving devices? Lay down
On your cold surface, the burden of mortal life, wheel-spoked, whirled.

Do your peaks and valleys simulate ups and downs, battle fatigued life?
The fickle fireflies, plunging into our abyss; then seek refuge in ashrams,
The beauty and the horror of the flesh, restore mental balance, fanned across
The flame, warmed by the gauzy light of your innards. Meditate.

On detachment, as your clear water tumbles down, renounce
The burdened, creeping holes of desire; bemoan the rotting roots, tear the
Shackles of the body; self purification begins in the strange languages
Heard, around you, dissolve, uprise, writhe, does sanyasa begin with you?

Why would your glacier-shaved forms invite austere inner courses?
To what end? You would strip the shaven heads of words, invite
Discord within the reaches of trust benign, gentle as your rolling vales,
A sacramental meeting with tapas, unblended, closures welling.

Stranded without contributions, none. A shaven head and
Flowing beard, stuck against your ageless mountain corridors,
Is *sanyasa* a way of self-purification, resonate like a hymn, humbling,
Does pilgrimage define you, or the crisscrossing paths of striving.

Does deliverance echo your forgotten, vast message in whispers?
Where does one deliver, free oneself in your barren lands isolated,
By massifs that dwarf ancient ways of being, disappearing rhythms,
Ancient trade routes, now almost gone, patterns of dying existence.

Whither a way of life, remote and impoverished, what connects?
The tapestry of non-attachment, struggle and survive, neither bitter
Nor joyous, a tapas way of life that seeks; give trust, nor consume it,
In messages holier than the shapes you represent, crawling high.

Why would we come to you to renounce, when your shapes multiply,
In the hushed silences of your ice-capped might? You dare connect
New bridges that stretch from earth to heaven, down the mystical,
Steep path, resonate with the spirit of conquering, a consciousness.

Born, transcend the expanding universe, ascend your heights,
The merciful gods beckon, for we see them better, more spectacular;
Your peaks, dusted with snow, or covered in elaborate show, a
Clear perspective, where in truth, our last steps lead us, onward.

What is left to overcome, squinting at your lofty observation
Site, let new adventures think what they want; you imply new Secrets.
An expansion begins as we wrap ourselves in your seeming
Purple and blue line of dashes, firm, still, constant as you. Sacred.

Once gazing at your verticality, like a stoplight of multiple
Centers, your sepia-toned colors adrift in the striving, centeredness,
Navel centered beings, high point of cosmic strength, if it means what
It means, your vertical bodies staring in silence. Eternal.

Prophesize, sacrifice, foreshadow. Your kind of prophecies
Carry an atmosphere of collaborative possibilities. Like a new
Path of dreaming, gleaming, unknowns; your heights a mirage,
Like sedately blossoming powers, page turning back, eternity unguarded.

Like eternity unguarded, you have worlds out there, sprout
Innumerable seeds, the bare spaces between your mountainous
Dreams, imply an unclipped sacrality; follow it always with your intent
Look, eyes that dare, your tumbling rocks cannot hold.

Your star stuck gaze is smeared with your milky white nipples,
Unslept with snow covered peaks, what nakedness stares down?
Is there an after-glow, like separate lives you would make us wince,
So much dignity, we too would rise. Or should.

Mountains of intention, what elaborate towers would you weave?
With the gesture of a dare, brilliant force of intention. Or is it
Invention? The fluidity of a golden eagle, what soaring heights
Would you move us toward, sage, or the virtue of what symbol?

NISHI CHAWLA is an academician and a writer. She holds a doctorate in English from The George Washington University, Washington D.C., USA.

Dr Nishi Chawla has taught for nearly twenty years at the University of Delhi, India. For the last two decades, she has been teaching English Literature in the US.

This is her fifth collection of poetry. In addition, she has published four volumes of poetry, two novels, and three plays.